Scarred

Beautifully Scarred
A True Journey through Abuse, Hurt, and Pain

by
Natasha Traceen Tolbert

Copyright © 2019 by Natasha Tolbert.

All rights reserved. No part of this book may be reproduced, scanned, or distributed in any printed or electronic form without permission.
The characters and events portrayed in this book are fictitious or exaggerated. Any similarity to real persons, living or dead, is coincidental and not intended by the author.

Published by BlackGold Publishing

First Edition: June 2019
Printed in the United States of America
Published by BlackGold Publishing
ISBN: 978-1-7337806-5-0

Dear Reader

This book is a compilation of my life expressed through poetry, and a short story of a real event that took place in my life that sparked the motivation to put it all together…

The pain expressed in this book is for Women everywhere that have been through traumatic relationships and /or Domestic Violence.

Table of Contents

About The Author
Dedications

Poems – (In the form of falling petals…)
Pages 1-102

Author's Notes

About The Author

Natasha Tolbert was born and raised in Staten Island, New York. She moved to Phoenix Arizona in 2001 fleeing from a domestic violence situation. She started writing to let out a lot of the pain that she has suffered in her life. As she wrote she realized how her thoughts turned into poetry, as she could not write it without it coming out like "songs from her heart", as she describes them. After she and her children were held hostage in 2011, she began to write more through therapy, and decided to tell her recall of events from that devastating day. She incorporated her poetry in this book to describe the hurt and pain that she has felt throughout her life. She continues to express how she feels through her writing. "Every day, I struggle through the pain that I have suffered..... not just from October 1, 2011 but from years of physical, sexual, and emotional abuse, brought on from the people who have claimed to love me. I am working to rebuild myself, as I have felt broken and damaged for so long…"

"I can say that out of all the pain that I have suffered, good things have come from it. The best and greatest of those things being my 5 beautiful children. They are the most Important, and have been my strongest supporters. I Love them more than anything!"

"I see my therapist regularly, and continue to work through my pain in my writing. Thank you for allowing me to share some parts of my pain, my hurt, my love, my soul….."

"…My Life."

Dedications

This book is dedicated to my children… Without them I would not have been able to make this journey, they are my strength. To women everywhere who have been abused, manipulated, battered, and worn…..
Who fight every day to keep it together and smile through the tears…..

"We Got This! Don't ever give up!"

And lastly – To Pain… To Hurt... To Love...
Thank you for the Inspiration.

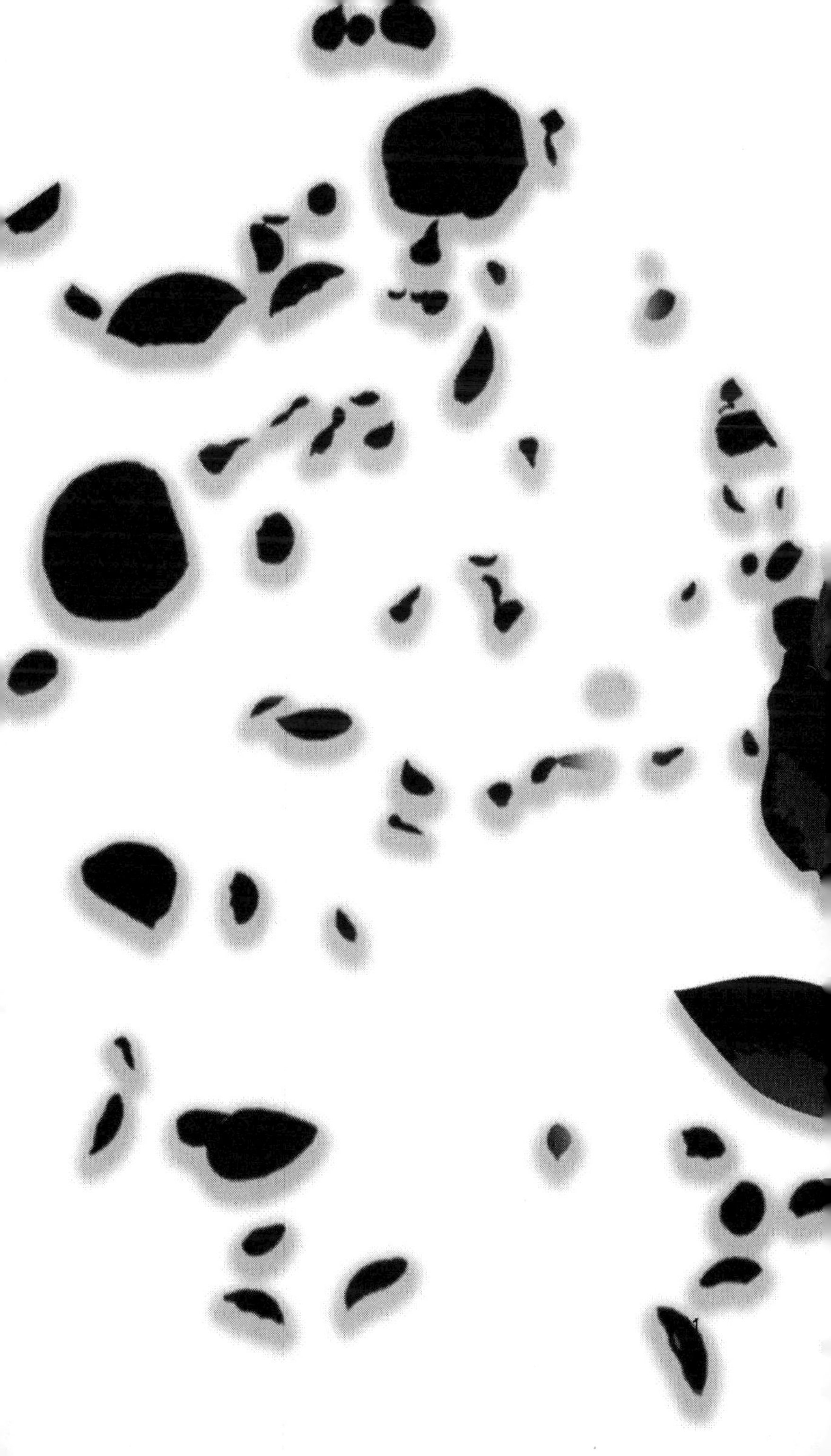

Why was I abused...?
As a child , as a teen , as an adult, as a woman...
Do I believe that sometimes I was deserving of the abuse... the chaos in my life... I do have a filthy mouth,... Can be very disrespectful. But I've been disrespected by many... hurt by many... lied by many...
In all relationships... friends... family... lovers... I love hard... and always give my all.

Still I hurt... Still I cry...
What's wrong with me?

Am I not deserving of Love and Kindness?
Am I worthy of anything?
Something good... something real...
Something all my own.....

Alcohol filled cups...
sleepless nights...

that turn into fist fights...
then red and blue lights...
Police reports, restraining orders piled in sneaker boxes and dresser drawers...
STD's brought on from those nasty hoes, and your unprotected ways... out in them streets...
gone for days and days...
Spit in my face... in front of my kids

you disgrace me...

Call me names, break my things. Steal my money... then leave me lonely...

"Nobody wants you...
you got 3 kids, and your busted."

I believed that shit too, when I think about it now... I feel so disgusted...
With myself mostly... for allowing someone like you to control me...

Please don't hit me no more... I don't know what I did so wrong to make you treat me like this... Please don't hit me no more... I will say sorry a thousand times... if you would just tell me what

They say love is not supposed to hurt...
but oh man what a lie
Busted lips, broken nose,
and curled up on the floor...

Beggin him to stop...
beggin please no more!...

Is this the man who took me under his wing... the same Fuckin one who said I was his everything?. Hold up , wait a minute, stop the fuckin music...
Rewind this shit...
Is this a fuckin scene
from a twisted movie clip?

Living in a nightmare, but I'm wide awake... My head feels so heavy, walking in a zombie state... Smother me with pillows to silence the sounds... "shut the fuck up Tash", he says as he pounds and he pounds. I feel myself slipping away... "Oh my God!", I think as I start to pray... Thoughts of my kids in my mind... I can't believe... this is not happening...

this can't be goodbye! I stop moving and quiet myself... can't believe this nigga, tryna send me to my death!

He gets up off of me, takes the pillow from my face... "Stupid bitch, get in the shower... you're a fuckin disgrace!" Whimpering and sore, I head towards the door, he grabs me by my arm... "say a fuckin word I swear I'll give you some more"

I cry silently in the shower, talking to the lord, asking him to free me... and what's this punishment for... I jump back in fear as he comes in the bathroom... handing me a towel... with tears in his eyes... he wraps his arms around me...

"Tash I'm so sorry, it won't happen again Tash, I promise, I swear".

I stand there wanting to say something... can't open my mouth... so swollen from the beating. Through clenched teeth I ask him why... I cry... He cries... But he gave no reply

Please don't hit me no more... I don't know what I did so wrong to make you treat me like this... Please don't hit me no more... I will say sorry a thousand times if you would just tell me what for.

I am Angry
I am hurt
I am distrustful
I am afraid

I am angry because I've seen things
I didn't deserve.

Things that I had no control over...
I am hurt because the people who were promised
to love me didn't...
I've been lied to and hurt some more...

So now, I don't believe the words...
I don't believe the promises...
Not falling for the lies...

Am I now hurting myself
by keeping my emotions inside.
Trying to save what's left of my heart...
You can't hurt me with your words...
With your promises...with your lies....
I'm no longer listening...

This is so unfair…
Why do I have to suffer so much?

My mom=no support
She doesn't even know me... has said she doesn't like me...and has shown that she doesn't care...

My dad=dead and gone…
Was gone before he died…never really got to know him…
Wish that could have been different...

How is it that your soul can hurt?

When will this pain inside go away?

Killing myself daily, with unreleased emotion, alcohol and smoking...

Not sleeping…negative thinking…

Will I be dead before I experience happiness?

Joy…Love…
Something good?

There will be someone who loves me…

All of me.
All the time…

To kiss me…hold me…touch me…
and wants only me…

I don't need your
inattentiveness…disinterest…..your arrogance
and sneakiness…

Fuck you!
You liar, you snake ass fake!

There is someone out there who will love me.

Every inch of me…..

Love me through my anger, love me through my
madness, and even through my crazy…

And I will be right there
to love all of him in return.

●

One day I will be ready... I will be free...
My heart will be open....to trust and believe that
Loving won't hurt me...
To learn on someone who won't push me away...
but pull me in closer and want me to stay... To
not be afraid to share all of me... no fear of
masking my emotions... to show off all scars on
the inside Beautifully...

●

Tears no longer
For you I won't hunger
Like a bulimic, I throw up the parts of you I
binged and craved for.....
Until my appetite for you is no more.....
Fasting now……

●

Save me from the lonely.....
I prayed for a soul that belongs to me only.....
Save me from the lonely.....
Two set of strong arms to pull me close,
And hold me.

●

What is life without Love...
Empty
Cold
Lonely
What is the point of making...?
Connections… Conversations. Interactions.
Without Love…. what is Life...?

●

Love is simple.....
It's people who are difficult
Love is constant.....
I need that.

●

Pick your poison.
Love or Hurt?
One of them has to be chosen.
Conflicted daily, so I try to do a tally.....
Love seems to not exist no more.....
Lust seems to be the things
with the highest score.
Never been one to follow suit.....
But me being in Love with Love gets me hurt.....
And with the way my heart set1up.
I'm loyal to a fault..... So I stay getting stuck.

●

Is it you..... or is it me?
Because if It's me,
I'm willing to fix, whatever it is.
Just so, We… Can…Be.....
And if It's you.....
Tell me what it is, that will help you be.....
That Man...
You want to be.
Anything is fixable. And anything is workable.
If it is where
You… Want... To... Be...
I'm here for you...
Are you ... here ... for... me...?
Your love language + My love language=
Our Love Language...

Are
You
Ready?

Why don't I understand my worth?
Is it something I created? Or from past experiences that got instilled in me on a quest to quench my thirst.
A thirst for love.....
My heart is dry like these desert sands.....
Desperate for a drink, I think is gonna be found in any man...
A touch... a hug... a kiss...
I settle for things like this.
But Love is what I'm longing for...
Or maybe I'm just unsure...
What am I worth?
A fake smile... fake words...
some dick to give me hope?
I always settle..... I need to know my worth.

Who the fuck wants to be surrounded by shade,
hate and superficial faces
Pretending to be this or that. When reality is
they're just taking up space

Running through life with fake smiles and false
beliefs to fit into a fucked up society where social
media rules all

Suicides, little girls half naked and twerking,
hating themselves so much they'd rather be
plastic and made by Mattell

Cheating spouses, side Becky's and slut bitches
being worshipped like the 9/11 building that
used to stand so tall

A dying race that nobody cares about
until It's one of their own...

Running mouths, lying lips, and a pointed finger
to place blame. just to gain a name.

I'm drowning in this place.

Save Me.

What is the purpose
of your presence in my life?
If It's not for us to be together.
What is the lesson I have to learn from these
feelings of bad weather?
Hell No!. I can't stand the rain...
If you didn't come to change the pain...
that I've always known.
So am I supposed to let go of the emotion...?
Or let go of you.

Let my emotions flow...?
I really just don't know...
I'm tired of feeling so confused...
And although I can't say
I necessarily feel used...,
It kind of sorta
Feels like the abuse...

That... I'm... used... to
.
I feel off balance and drunk without drinking
Going with the flow of things
without even thinking...
Of what this whole situation...
Is... doing... to... me
How It's..... affecting..... me.
Why were you brought in my life...?
If you weren't supposed to stay...
Why do people come in...,
and then just go away…?

Trying to force someone to be more, or to give more than they are capable of, is unfair and not real. I guess my decision to allow my emotions to take over... somehow needed to happen... It freed me and it freed him. I think It's probably better this way. He won't feel pressured, and I won't feel that unwanted or unimportant feeling that has been nudging at me for so long. Trusting him, but then again, not really trusting him. Feeling resentful and hurt. That's not the way to love anyway. Maybe I never really loved him. Maybe it was just the idea of him. The excitement of him... the familiarity of him. Lusting mostly for his body and his hands on mine. Fear of a loneliness that was always there. Not wanting him touching anyone else. When I already felt he was doing when not with me. That's not love after all. I thought I could handle the pieces of him that he chose to give me, when he wanted to give it to me... But deep down... I wanted all of him, and settled for just a piece. Late night hours... and mostly I was ok to lay with him through the night. It just wasn't enough. I didn't feel I was enough... and in many ways he made me feel like I wasn't enough. Got tired of expressing this to him, and feeling that way. Him never feeling he needed to explain anything, and rightfully so I guess... because he wasn't mine. Wasn't mine to ask for an explanation... wasn't mine to expect anything but whatever he chose to give me. And me afraid to not have any part of him…

●

Reaching and Reaching.
Searching for something
or searching for nothing
Empty and emptier still
Lonelier and Alone still.....

●

All around me I see unfamiliar faces.
Voices sound the same, but I can't place a name
And my heart becomes filled with
yet more empty spaces.....
Maybe the problem is me.....
And I just can't see.

Or maybe the masks have fallen off of who they
all pretended to be.

I'm still dealing.....

I'm empty.
I'm cold

It's been going on too long.
And this… this "thing."
Is getting old.
And the Love, that I Love.....
Is really starting to feel.....
Nothing, like Love...
Because, I mean, if Love is what I want...
If Love is what I give...
If Love is what I am...
Shouldn't he...?
Shouldn't we...?
Just... Be...?
Why won't he...?
Just...
Love... Me...?

What if one day, I have nothing left to give...
Nothing left to say...?
What will he do...?
What will I do...?
If I can no longer stay…

Daddy, I miss you.
I miss what I knew and all the things
I didn't get to know.
Apparently, we're a lot alike...
Or that's what I've been told.
If that's a good or bad thing...
is something I'll never know...
I miss you Daddy...
The parts of you that I knew... and the parts...
I'll never get to know.

Tick tock, Tock tick
As the hands of time go by and by.....
The seasons changing over and over again.
She continues to look through dark windows
with black drapes.
For something or someone to bring back
the pieces of her heart...
Her eyes are fierce and her face is stern.
Smiling on the outside..... dying within.....
Small sparks of hope flutter by with flirtations
from small whispers in the air...
Still... no one comes... at least not to stay...
So she writes off those pieces...
and pretends not to care.

●

I cry inside..... My emotions I hide.....
To show that I'm hurt...
I will never abide.

Sometimes I avoid eye contact,
so you cannot see...
The pain that I hold inside of me.....

To allow the tears to fall is like a bullet in a
chamber..... the thought of it alone.....
brings about so much anger...

A dangerous thing... these fuckin emotions...

I scare myself with the racing thoughts that play
over and over...
Like a hit song on heavy rotation...

My reality is like nothing you'd EVER know.....
And I promise you,
It's somewhere you'd NEVER wanna go…

I came across this drug
and I regret it every day...
There wasn't a meeting or rehab that could help
me recover...

I relapsed on this drug over and over…

The blissful, mind altering, invigorating affects,
takes a hold of your soul...
On a trip so high, you no longer have control...
Your thoughts... your feelings...
are no longer your own.
Floating and soaring, body is tingling...
smiling to yourself...
Caught in a world that nothing can reach...

The day comes and this drug is no more..., not
cuz you can't find it, or no longer a fiend...
It's been ripped away by something unseen...
You crash so hard, you're now cold,
angry and bitter...
Sad, lonely, there's no consoling.....

Shaken and weakened, the light leaves from your
eyes, and your heart just stops beating...

This drug…L~O~V~E.

It Killed Me.

Dear self…
Look at how far you've come… I bet you thought you wasn't gonna make it.
But you did...
We did...
It's been a long hard journey, and It's not over, no way….
Not even close.

I know you think back to all the bullshit that was supposed to stop you, break you, damn, take your life. Obstacle after obstacle, heartbreak after heartbreak. Yours still standing. There are always going to be bad days, but compared to all you suffered thru, you should be able to smile through those bad days..... well at least smirk, I know how you don't smile often. But you should, you have a lot to smile at, a lot to be thankful and grateful for.
So work on that.....

My heart is coming back together. I'm not afraid anymore. Afraid for what/ I have faced the worse of the worse... I am the strongest woman I know, and so are you.

You gotta believe it though. I don't know
what happened...,

I woke up one day and just decided
not to be afraid of life!!
That's who I am, I am all of those things...
So all this time
I've been afraid of myself... Fuck that.

I love me. I love you! We are who we are
because of all the things that was
supposed to break us, to stop us, to kill
us!! I'm not going to give up on life, or on
love. I deserve to be happy, and
I deserve to be loved.
We, deserve to be loved! And I still gotta
whole of love to give,
and a whole lotta living to do.

So do you. So let's get it! I got you, and
you got me! We haven't let each other
down yet, so you ready to claim whats
ours? What we know
we rightfully deserve?

We are Unbreakable, and Unstoppable...

Take my hand....

Good morning beautiful
I was thinking about you
I really wanna see you

Can I cum thru.?

Damn... You drive me crazy...
I miss you.

Morning Beautiful
Such a beautiful soul...
I want you in my life... in the future...
Youre so strong...
I'm sorry... I'll never hurt you like that again.
Pinky promise
It's not like that.

Morning.
Don't nobody want that girl.
I can't explain it
It was only, like twice.
Stop, don't act like that!
I belong to no one...
Don't be so negative.
I really just need time to know myself...
I fell asleep
I'm just really busy...
nothing like how you think.
Here we go...
SO sexy. Damn. You drive me fuckin crazy...
I can't give you what you want at this time.
I don't want anything or no one.

You better not be giving away my good stuff...
Sorry… just been busy, I'll try...
WYD Sexy...?
I wanna see you
I always miss you, I just don't tell you.....
Sorry...I'm just busy... that's all
Is it still all mine...?
I still talk to her from time to time…, but It's not like that.
I can't help the way you think.
Why would I tell you to come over and not answer...? I fell asleep...,
Just really exhausted.
I'm not in the mood to deal with the attitude
Hey Sexy...WYD, how's my juicy fruit doin?
You're too much for me... I can't hang...
Just busy, that's all
Hey you.
It's not like that at all
Will you stop!
Hey Love.....
Miss you muaah.
I'll see you soon
Dam, I'm just busy, working and all, sooo not in the mood
Very soon, you gonna squirt for me...?
I'll try... I should be able to
Not gonna be up all night
with your crazy ass either.
Just got a lot going on
We are not together tho...
I don't have to lie, or explain anything to you...
"WYD Sexy...?"

Fucckin whirliwind of emotional turmoil
Spinning me out of control...

AGAIN!! Picking up pieces of my broken soul...
Muthafucka you come into my life just to turn it
upside down Who the fucck do you think you
are to treat people that way
Using your charm and sexuality pretending to be
a good guy When you just tell half truths and
misuse, and throw people away...

You fucckin bastard, you make me sick and I
make myself even sicker
for not knowing better than you

Wanting better than you
Deserving better than you
You, who just manipulate me with just the
simplest shit,
From your lying lips
That I love to kiss

So I wasn't even listening, just watching your
mouth move and thinking about sticking my
tongue...inside...of...your...mouth.

When It's probably been on every woman we
both know… And you and I both know that
they're not better than me...

She's not better than me...

And nigga you know, with your trifilin ass that, I was the best you ever had...and now I'm the best you never had... even though. I actually never had the chance to be....with…you…like that...other than for sex.

Which was...the greatest sex, I ever had...and now is the greatest sex youll never have, or ill ever... have...again... Oh My God! I'm so angry right now! I can just wrap my hands around your neck... And my legs around your back, while you dig deeper...
into my already fucked up heart...

Which YOU broke again! By the way muthafucka, and then said whateva...
So now It's forget it foreva...and fuck this crazy love shit... and who the fuck said it was love... or is it love that's making me crazy...or am I crazy, In Love...Or Am I just…Crazy...?

●

You cut me in half
And throw away and ridicule the parts of me
That are not beneficial to you
You cut me in half
With words of disappointment
That makes my insecurities feel like contentment.
Settling and smiling though it all
As you cut me in half
Strong and withstanding more
Crying, screaming, and unraveling inside.
Suffocating with pillows of deception and lies
But Now, that you cut me in half...
I realize, I'm Imperfectly me.
And the other half that
I thought I needed was you.
And those pieces ... those pieces...
That YOU threw away...
Can no longer be put back together...
And I guess MY pieces will be missing
from you...
Forever...

●

You can't love me
the way you Love everybody else...
You can't Love me halfway...
Half the time...

Sleeping with the enemy

Delusions
Illusions
Loving me
Hating me
Hurting me
Wanting me
Holding on
Letting go
Conflicted
Afflicted
Lies and deceit
Lingering kisses
Days of disappearances
No sign of the I Miss You

I love hard and always pay the price
with my heart...
Shattered again...
Because I believe in your words...
I constantly wonder… will I ever find someone...
To really Love... Me.
To feel the love that I give so deep and freely...
To never walk away... stay close infinitely
Love is all I want
And HIS heart...
I'd die for it...
Does he feel my love...?
Is it love that he wants...?
Does He have it to give...?
To me...?
To have a bond so deep...
Late night sessions... all about everything discussions.
Argue and then agree to disagree...
Then make love passionately...
Does he even hear me... when I say…
"I Love You"
Maybe I'm not enough...
Maybe he's not enough...
Maybe love is not for him...
Maybe I'm not for him
Emotionally incompatible
But sexually... My God, we're incredible...
I crave for your touch... that insatiable feeling...
And then try to rationalize with myself, on Why...

Deception only in the eyes of me...
The things you said were never truth to see...
I only believed what I wanted it to be.
Sad it is,
that my ignorance to what love means to you...
Is..., or was not,
the vision of my happiness with you.
The respect and the integrity I had was true...
The way things are now... brings it all back...
The hurt and pain I felt so long ago...
But as I think about it... It's never went away...
Really thought you wouldn't do me that way...
The only thing promised was...
that I would stay...
And you...
you just never felt that way...

●

When did you stop seeing me?
Me... for more than just a pretty face...?
When did you stop seeing me?
Me... as your friend...
Your go to when you were at your lows and just needed ... ME
Makes me wonder
if you ever really looked at me...
Looked into me...
I showed you ME
I taught you ME
I gave you... ME
The darkest of me
The pain and the hurt of me...
The crazy, emotional and most vulnerable... ME
When did you stop seeing me?
When did you stop needing me?

Waited and waited for something to change
Held on and let go, then held on some more
Still... things never went back
to the way they were before
Movin on was something I never wanted to do
Had to face it, my love... just wasn't for you
Your walls are too high for me to climb
As I sent away the guards from my heart...
You, sent for more to block me from yours.....
Distant…
And then the silence grew us further apart.....

Messages and calls from you consistently only when I don't respond.....
Any other time I get excuses
of why you abscond.
The love you say you have for me...
Shows up when I silently set you free...
Ignored text messages and now,
your doing phone calls...
When the things I request is so small
Respect, honesty, and friendship that's all...
Apparently what I ask is too much to provide
You've lied, treated me like nothing...
Left me alone in court room to plead falsely and testify...
Against a chick you claimed was a "Nobody."
Which low key.....
I can't get past.
And was that last... straw for me.
I express my feelings and It's "oh boy", and the "here we go"
Making it seem like I'm the problem, and I'm the one that needs to grow...
I've been understanding
I've been patient, I respect your space and I've always been translucent
When I decide not to respond to your texts or calls. The only thing you can come up with is...
I must have, or am fuckin someone else...
Because obviously, it can't just be YOU are the problem.

●

It's really time to stop fooling myself
Nothing is changing but the days and the time
Life is moving forward, and we are not
What I want, is clearly not what you're about
That day will never come
when you will be all mine
It's funny how when I'm mad, or find out
something you've done
You get consistent and try to convince me that
I'm the only one
I believe you...
And you fall right back into habit...
Disappearing like a magician does a rabbit
Then I start looking desperate,
tryna get your attention
Sending you pictures, or constantly textin...
There you go with the reasons and excuses about
your schedule
The "I'm sorry",
of how you really wish you could see me...
Buuut...
Just a number in the rotation,
and it just not my turn
I don't even wanna think about
how many there might be
But to be the only one
I obviously have not earned...
So no matter how I feel...
. I've already come to see
I just gotta let it Burn.

Drawn to you
The same ole you
Manipulation never sounded so sweet
My own insecurities never felt so good
As long as it was coming from your lips
Hating you, but loving you at the same time
Drawn to you
That same ole you
The same words
I hear from different mouths...
Still soothe me in those same insecure places
In different tones
Still, I'm drawn to the same ole you
Lost in a world where truth
and loyalty doesn't exist
Pain and lust is all to be found
With nowhere to turn
I'm drawn to the same ole ...YOU

Is it my time...? My time to let you go...?
I've stayed consistent with my feelings...
But now,
I don't think I have anything left to show...
I know in love there are no limits...
I've done my part to remain close...
But for you... You, keep that doors... Closed.

●

3 years...
And nothing is what I meant...
And how dare I think that I did...
I mean the messages were sent…
and sent... and sent
Silly of me, I guess I just didn't get it.

Continuously tossed on the sideline...

For whatevea or whoeva.
Who the hell did I think I was...

To believe that you were all mine…?
I mean you said it a time or two...
But never followed up
with things you said you'd do

With your untouchable heart, your untouchable emotions
Me, reaching for something with an untouchable notion.

3 years...
how dare I think that I meant anything...
I guess somehow in my mind...
havin a little bit of something...

Was better than not having anything...
but still ended up with...

Nothing...

●

A lover who hides from his own heart
Disguising and hiding
from the most beautiful part...

Himself mostly...

I wonder sometimes if he gets lonely...
It must be those times
when he uses pieces of me...

And I give it to him...

Freely, deeply
Passionately...humbly... and truly...
Ending things
before something can even start...
Tiptoeing around emotions...
Advertently avoiding any notion of care...
Pushing away any thoughts of having someone
permanently there...
Never ready for anything more that the situation
at the time...

If you try and get close...
He will... leave you behind...

A lover who hides from his own heart...

I have risked all of myself…

No matter how foolish…

Just for a little piece of you…

●

Fuckin whirlwind of emotional turmoil spinning me out of control...

Again! Picking up the pieces of my broken soul

Muthafucka you come in my life just to turn it upside down Who tha fuck do you think you are to treat people that way?!

Using your charm and sexuality, pretending to be a good guy... When all you tell is half-truths and misuse and lead them astray...

You fuckin bastard you make me sick!
And I make myself even sicker for not knowing better than you

Wanting better than you
Deserving better than you

You, who just manipulates me with just the simplest shit from your liyin lips...

That I love to kiss

So I wasn't even listenin, just watchin your mouth move and thinkin about stickin my

Tongue inside...
Of...your...mouth...
When It's probably been...
on...every woman we both know...

And even I know that they're not bettah than me!
She's not betta than me!
And even you know... with your triflin ass that I was the best you ever had, and now I'm the best you never had...

Even though I actually never had the chance to be with you...other than for SEX!

Which was the greatest sex...I've ever had, which is now the greatest sex you'll never have or... I'll ever...have...again...

Oh My God! I'm so angry right now! I can just wrap my hands around your neck...

And my legs around your back...while you dig deeper into...
My already fucked up heart...

Which you broke AGAIN!...
by the way Muthafucka!

And then said whateva...
so now It's forget it forevaa...
And Fuck this crazy love shit... and who the fuck said that it was love anyway...

Am I just crazy in love...? or is this love shit makin me crazy...?
Or am ... I... just...

Crazy…?

Although I knew how it would all end...

I continued to play,
while you continued to pretend...

As if there was really
a future for us...
So many things you would say, and
in your words, I wanted to trust...
And hoping that you'd stay...

Deep down I always felt,
there was no winning your heart...

Trying to compete with someone
who has such a hold on your soul...
But the way you made me feel...
I had no control...

I should have left it alone from the
first time you lied...
I tried to let go...
I tried... I really tried...
But my mind couldn't escape, the
way you had me fired up inside…

I put myself in these situations...

need to know my worth...
Self-esteem...anger...and pain
Keep me from positive gain...

Colder I become...have no one to blame...
And no matter how used and ashamed...

I continue to reach for things too far from my grasp...
a lot of it stems from my past...
So again
I say goodbye to yet another...
Semi-Part time lover...

Pieces of my heart
he takes with him...
And the hurt and the pain I hide...
and keep, deep within...

If I stop talking to you...
I'll have to stop thinking about you...

If I stop thinking about you...
I'll forget about you...

If I forget about you...I'll never see you again...

Who am I to you?

What can't I say... what can I do...?

What are we doing...?

Can't take a picture...
can't be seen anywhere...

My feelings are hurt...
can't help how I feel about you…

So lonely…

●

You came in her store and liked what you saw... and you tried it all on... To see if it fit, and if it was something you could rock wit... On a regular basis—maybe even on special occasions...You have a lot of priorities, so you weighed your options... Felt like you needed to ask questions...think on it some more—so you know if the quality... is right for you...at this moment... at this time... However, you decided you would put a lil' something down...have it held for you, until you got in the right state of mind... Day after day you'd come back in... tryin the same thing on...diggin the fit...lovin it more, but still couldn't commit... To makin the Entire purchase...Still... you would leave a little more and say "thank you" for her service... "don't give it away", you'd leave and say... "I want that, and It's gonna be mine one day." She smiled at him, and said her good-bye... Always on her mind if he'd ever pay full price...

"I'll keep it for for you,
don't worry, you got it"...
"It's all yours when you ready...I promise."

As the seasons changed...he came in less and less... sometimes leaving nothing for the cashier drawer ring... She wondered what had happened... What might have changed his mind so. Had he found something better... in another storefront window?... More time would pass...and he hadn't come in... didn't receive a single dollar... for what she hid from others... "No sale on this item" She'd say and turn away

46

their cash... One day she sat, looked over the
receipts... She recalled the payments already
received... As she counted it up,
and did the math...
she realized that it wasn't even half...
She hung her head...
and laughed and laughed...

But only to herself...cuz she felt like such a
fool...she had to play it off because to everyone
else she's too cool... He comes around still... every
now and then...putting down the smallest
amount...says he doesn't have much to spend...
Says he has a lot going on, and priorities
changed...At that very moment she finally
realizes...what she's been keeping only for
him...he will never come to claim ...

"Layaway Love"

-Pocket Chic-
You keep me in the pocket of your favorite jeans... The jeans you put on when nothing is clean... Like that crumpled up dollar you find, when you need it for tax...

I run when you call, and you know I'll be there, no questions asked...

Irrelevant, until that day comes when your laundry not done and have nothing to wear...

Hanging on the back of a chair...
your favorite jeans...

And in your pocket…you'll find me there...

Being in love is like music to my ears.
The beautiful sounds of hearts racing and going pound... pound...
Not sure if I've gone deaf or if someone turned it down... Because I can't hear...
Not a jingle… a whistle... not a single beat...
I see people around me
sashaying and swaying...

And it feels like I've lost my rhythm...

Not even a two-step from these feet...
I'm missing the soulful nights of the quiet storm playing. The butterflies inside and smiling all the time...

Holding hands and slow kissing...
staying up all night...

Talking…reminiscing...

I can't hear the music of...

L-O-V-E

●

Let me in

I won't hurt you

Let me in

My heart is true

Let me in

I just want to love you...

●

My heart is hopeful ...
to love again...
For Forever...
Not just for a moment...
I will hear those words out loud...'
Not in a whisper...
I Love You...
I see LOVE in my dreams...
Waiting just to take me...
LOVE is... waiting for Me.

Embraces like fine wine… Sweet.

Although some of our dances have been bitter...

None the less,

You are the answer to every silent fantasy.
Your lips respond with the most tender...

Love making with you is chemistry in action...

Sensuality at midnight... rocking and holding on with erotic pleasure...

Nothing can measure...

●

One day I will be ready... I will be free...
My heart will be open... to trust and believe that
Loving won't hurt me...To lean on someone who
won't push me away...but pull me in closer and
want me to stay…To not be afraid to share all of
me…no fear of masking my emotions…

To show off all of my scars on the inside…

Beautifully…

●

They say nothing real can be threatened
But the things you do threaten every feeling
I ever had for you
The lies you told
The love you said was mine
Threatened time after time
How can that be real...?
You give me some of you...
Then take away more
Confused now on
if the parts you give are true...
Threatened now is
everything we've ever shared

So how could it have ever been real...?

Spend too much time
trying to convince you I'm good enough

Honest enough

Loyal enough

Worthy enough

While you play games and open your mouth with empty words that have no intention

Other women...

A bundle of excuses

Roller coaster ride of emotions
Or lack there of
Spent too much time wondering why...

I'm not good enough

Worthy enough

Picking myself apart,
tryna see what I could do better
How can I be better...?
to be able to fit in your world

Be good enough for you

Then one day something happened
I opened my eyes and woke up from this
bad dream I kept having about myself...

Realizing... maybe… just maybe...
You... were not...

Good enough

Honest enough

Loyal enough

Or worthy enough

For Me.

Stay you say...

Stay so you can continue to inhale me
and get your fix of me...
Stay...until you grow bored of me and you need
to see if someone else gets you the same
high...then call me back after realizing you just
might lose me this time...

Stay... you say...

Stay, so you can fall back
into who you really are....
Manipulate my thoughts and make me believe
It's just me...and It's always been me... and
nothing is worth losing me...

Stay... you say...

Stay, while you entertain yourself with whoever
else on the days you're not feeling so sure of
yourself and need attention...

Stay... you say

While you continue the lies and excuses and flip
flop your emotions from one day to the next...

Stay... you say

But dare I bring up any infractions or my hurt
feelings and just stay that cool down ass Tash...

"let's start over" you say
"I do love you" you say
"I thought you knew that" you say

When nothing you do
shows that and nothing has changed...
And the only thing still happening… on
occasion... is Sex...

No meaningful conversations...none of your
actions have changed...

I'm hearing the same old thing…

"I'm just misunderstood" you say.

While never expressing what it is , o
r what you want... or don't want...

"don't take your love from me" you say

The love you take for granted
The love you don't know how to receive.
The love you don't know how to give
The love you don't deserve

Stay...you say...

Why should I...?
Why do I...?

●

The love I have for you
doesn't protect you no more

                        The connection...
              our connection is so strong...

I can't take it anymore

         The intuition I have...
      I just can't shake it no more...

                 When we fuck now,
           and you say It's the best...

      I can't help but to think
      you say the same to all the rest...

I feel your lies...
and I see it in your eyes...

                 And who we were...
              or what I thought...

      I just can't care anymore...
      The friendship, the trust...
      It's just not there no more...

The man I loved a
and thought I knew...
He's just not there anymore...

            I'm Gone.

●

Urgently always running to you...

Afraid of someone else doing the things I do...

Turns out there was always a reinforcement to fill in whether I ran or not

Blindly trusting that you would never let someone in my spot...

Irreplaceable... Unforgettable...

Oh how silly of me to think that...

Off and on

On and off

Like a light switch you turn me
I fall back
You run towards me at full speed
Confessing your love
But never your bad deeds
Believing your own lies
Hiding behind excuses and alibis
Saying just enough to get me back

Where you want me
Giving you the side eye now,
and don't even realize

You don't even see,
That I'm low key just done
About to be off you
Enough is enough Son
Vibrating different now
I don't even know you now

Switch me on

Switch me off

You… My nigga…
Are gonna need a new light bulb…

●

He hasn't changed…
He just feels guilty…

●

The fact that I let you off,
Is just as bad as being a jump off

>You only show you care
>when I'm ready to step off

Sorry, but not sorry
 only cuz you got caught

>Lie after lie…
>without a care of worry

Your lies affect lives
and what makes it even sadder…

>Is that you continue
>these rifts and no one else matters

●

"Only when we know and recognize our own darkness within, can we be present with the darkness of others...
Compassion becomes real when we recognize our shared humility and humanity"

(excerpt from the book
"I Thought It Was Just Me, But It Isn't")

#COURAGE

●

Nights like this...

Thug passion

We smashing

Me on you

You on me

Fuckin the whole night thru

Bodies thrashin

Sweat splashin

Mind games and nicknames

Will pass on to the next flame

Fly by nights

Flirtatious days

Nasty texts

That lead to freaky sex

Reminisce, cuz you gonna miss

nights like this.

Let's talk...

Tell me you don't want me
the way I want you...

Tell me that you're selfish
and you have to have it all your way...

Tell me that It's not just me and that you juggle
between a lot of different women
for different reasons...

Tell me that you don't really love me, but you say
it because you think
that's what I wanna hear...

Tell me the real reason you put in more effort
when I'm ready to walk away from you, is
because you don't like rejection, and your pride
and ego is your biggest flaw...

I'll listen…
and then you can be the one to say...

Goodbye...

He says...

"Fuck wit me... let me show you what it is to be treated like the queen that I believe you to be"

She says...

"there's a lot you don't know about me, and I'm not ready to share"

He says

"your eyes say enough and I can see the hurt even through your smile, you don't have to share, but you don't have to hide... Fuck wit me and you'll smile again from the inside"

She's hesitant and resistant.
Fixated on the past and unhealed wounds that she carries. It won't allow her to move on to anything good. She's quiet and still...

He says...

"Stay with me" ...

"Let me fill that emptiness with nothing less than love and kindness, I see the handle with care sign. what will it take to ease your mind?'

She looks at him from the side, and says...

"what do you want from me...?"

"I have nothing left to give,
there are pieces of me walking around in
strangers that I used to know. whatever is left I
have to keep for myself"

He says…

"fuck wit me"

"I want to give you everything I have"
"I want to make you whole again"
"What do I want from you...?" He smiles

"I want your hurt"
"I want your pain"
"I want your tears and all your fears"
"give it to me…"

She drops a single tear...
He wipes it away...

She says...

"if I give you all of those horrible parts of me...
what would that do for you...?

He says...

"It will make room for you
to receive all the love I have..."
"fuck wit me"

Remembering the good times
The truthful times
The laughter shared
The good times

●

I Imagine a life filled with Strawberry kisses
Whispers of love
Passion unlimited
Cherished moments of truth and laughter
Embracing the unknown of happily ever after
I Imagine a life of break ups to make up

Because without the other one
it just won't add up

Binging on the scent of skin on skin
Intertwining becoming one beautiful soul in a
world full of hate and sin
Loving and loving until the end

Conquering all
Love wins

So if I let go

Will you let go too?

I mean like really let go...

Not the "she's trippin right now, I'ma give her a minute'... let go. But just let go...?

When I let go It's always intentional...
No time... no room...over emotional...
That's your story.

I let go

You say No

But why?

What do you want?

What is the purpose?

●

What is life without Love?
What is life without wanting
something more than nothing?
What is life without sharing it with someone
amazing and who makes you feel alive,
not empty and alone...?
I know the world is full of amazing
and beautiful people...
I just want ONE...
One who feels like I do… and loves like I do...

●

I fall in love with the chaos
The mess and the disaster inside
Because this is what I know to be true.

●

Erasing the emotions out of me
Silencing the screams
of someone please love me
Forgetting the love that never was
You're welcome to those who are walking
around with the stolen pieces of me
But, Fuck you for leaving me broken

●

Wake up
Wake up
Wake up
Girl what's wrong with you
You just gonna sleep through alarm clocks, stop lights and do not enter signs
How many lessons do you have to learn you wake up at the right time?
And get in the right line
The loving you and your life line
The you're beautiful you deserve better line
Wake up
Wake up
Wake up

●

Silencing the screams
of someone please love me
Forgetting the love that never was
You're welcome to those who are walking around with the stolen pieces of me
But, fuck you for leaving me broken

●

You look at me and all you see is responsibility.
Pretty...
Sexy...
Some ask why I don't have anyone of my own
Too much responsibility
I demand respect and honesty
Apparently, that's too much
Responsibility
I'm desired
I'm a fantasy
I'm fuckable
But too much of a responsibility.

●

Cowering to my insecurities

Enclosed like an envelope
marked return to sender

Compliments unaccepted
from anyone who may render

A kind word spoken
or even written on a letter unopened.

●

People don't grow apart
People stop being honest
and stop putting in effort
People start wondering about what could happen
with someone else.

●

I'm screaming, but nobody hears me
The worst pain in the world is...
Loneliness and rejection
Love is like air…
And I cannot breathe.

●

Just because the steps were different...
Doesn't mean that the walk in life wasn't the
name.
Create
Inspire
Motivate

●

Livin it
Lovin it
Hatten it
We in it

Life...

Rich in it
Poor in it
Struggling in it
We living this

Life...

Sad in it
Happy in it
Depressed in it
Moving though it

Life...

Real wit it
Fakin in it
Ready to be done with it

LIFE.

●

Shouldn't I be able to move forward with positive endeavors...?
Why should I have to relieve the feelings of torture and defeat...
The same things that could have or should have knocked me off my feet...
I'm a survivor who never accepts defeat
Oh, but this ache. This ache that haunts me daily to just achieve some type of normalcy...
Is never ending and Its low key
KILLING ME!

●

When the pain is so deep
Your secrets you can no longer keep
Reality sets in...
And you're now at the point of breakin...
What do you do?
Allow it and just succumb too...
Everything you've avoided
for years and years...
Let it out and just drown in the tears,
the tears, the tears...
The physical pain that brings back the old memories of the past...
Comes full force and have no idea of
how long it will last...
I'm scared now
I don't want to feel this now...
I really don't need this now...
I honestly can't take this now...

● ● ●

This section was written by the author and is a direct journal entry from her life and has been kept raw and edited for those reasons.

October, 1, 2011
Saturday morning~

Cooking breakfast... (eggs, toast)
~phone is ringin...Shottas on the T.V.
Friend, (jerry) on the couch...
I answer the phone. (Shanika hysterical, crying...
I don't understand...
Her boyfriend gets on the phone... says Shanika told him her dad was in the house @5am, walking around with a pillow and a gun...said she convinced him to leave... she left really early that morning...It's her birthday...apparently her dad dropped her off at a boyfriend's house...
"promised" her he wasn't going to hurt anybodya... I hang up…....call him…
Curse him out... "Wtf nigga, you was in my fuckin house'. With a fuckin gun muthafucks! Oh, so you a killah now, nigga! Fuck you clown! Kill yourself!"

I hang up

Akil~ "what happened ma? He was in the house with a gun?"

"Yeah, this bitch probably let him in, how the fuck he get in…no wonder she was up so early…fuckin sneaky little bitch!
This nigga has really lost his fuckin mind!"
I'mani-comes from her room.
"Can I go for walk?"
"No, you don't need totake a walk right now!"
Well, I'm gonna go feed the dogs"
She goes out back.
Najah-wandering around…
sound the house playing- Me-feeding Nailah in her boucny…
Talking going on…He comes in…
"everybody shut tha fuck up right now!
Me-nigga wtf you doin in my fuckin house, you fuckin clown, get the fuck out my house nigga, Stoopid ass,
Akil-"Ma shut up, shut up ma! Ma, Shut the fuck up this is not a game!"
Me- looking at Akil cursing at me "What"?
Me-looking back at him, "yea It's not a game-gun pointed at me.
"Wha happen, eh, talk yuh shit now eh"
Walks across the room head butts me hard.
Me-"Dave what you doin!? You don't have to do this'.
Him-picks up Najah…Kisses her…"Sup babes, youh good?" kisses her again.
@ Jerry…"and you muddafucka…wuh tha fuck youh doin in mi house?, I'mma kill yu first'
Jerry- "look man, I don't have nothing to do with what you guys have goin on man"
Him-"wha yu have behind ya back, trow it ova dere"
Jerry tosses cell phone to the other couch…
Doorbell rings…It's my nephew…
He answers…

"not right now Jamiel, yu don' need to be here right now man, I love you"...closes the door
"you stand up muthafucka, you da first to go..."pointing gun @ Jerry
Jerry- "you, what the fuck man,what you doin"...
Jerry flips up air mattress that was on the floor...
Him- pulls trigger...Jerry- jumps through window... glass shattering
Everybody screamin!!!
Gun doesn't go off, gun not cocked
"luck muddafucka, hmm, his big ass can run to nah, watch..."
I'mani-tries to sneak past and run in the room...
He grabs her throws her on the couch next to me...
She's crying...She's scared… Me too...
Akil- "Rudy you don't have to do this, I always looked at you like you was my dad,I don't reall know my real dad like that"
Him...Holds gun to his own head...
"Don't try that reverse psychology shit on me !"
@I'mani- "You! This shit is all ya fault, tell yuh muddah dat yu lie, I nevuh touch you, why yuh lie?"
I'mani-" I didn't lie , I felt you touching me, I'm not lying"…
Sound of helicopters...he looks out the window...
Makes us all go into the bedroom, barricades the door with the dresser… ties up Akil,
"I'm gonna kill you first, get in the bathroom…Stand in tha shower"...,
Pointing the gun... me screaming, I'mani screaming. He just closes the shower door.
The phone is ringing...He is pacing... Picks up Najah, still waving the gun….Nailah asleep in the bed... Me and I'mani sittin on the bed.

Me-"let the kids go Dave, ill leave with you... We can go wherever you want...Lets just go...Me and you"...
Him-"I don't fuckin trust you no more...You took away my family..."
The phone is still ringing, sound of helicopters still in the air.
Him-"Answer da phone, tell 'em I left"
Me- "hello...No...he's not here anymore....he left...ok...let me put some clothes on...
I hang up the phone
"they want us to come out Dave, one at a time, or they're gonna come in"
"Fuck dat, nobody leavin di house, we all gonna die today"
"Dave, please just let the kids go , Please!"
Him-sIt's on the floor, holds gun to his own head, whimpering.
Phone is ringing some more...
He stands up, hands me the phone.
Me- "yes we are gonna come out now"...
He hands me Najah,
Tells I'mani to get on her knees by the bed, Akil still in the bathroom.
Him-puts gun to the back of I'mani's head
"if we go to that door and police come tru here I'm gonna shoot everybody"
Me-*crying...* "Please Dave, stop this"
He moves the dresser away from the door enough for me, him, and Najah to leave the room.
Puts the gun to the back of my head now, turns to I'mani
"yuh bedda not fuckin move or make a fuckin soun"
Me-*crying*
Him-to me, with the gun to the back of my head ...pushes it against my head

"Go, Now, move!"

Walking behind me to the front door with the gun to my head the whole time.

"if we open this door, if I see police, I'm gonna shoot you , nah, open the door!"

Me holding Najah to my chest, not touching the door.

Him- 'Open tha door nuh!"

Me still not touching the door crying , holding my baby girl close to my chest

"please, Dave, Please No"

He reaches around me opens the door, I close my eyes tight , squeeze Najah tighter , I'm holding my breath, Scared, soo scared, shaking.

He nudges me forward with the gun still to my head.

I open my eyes, I see nobody, nothing.

A police car waaaay at the end of my street. I wave my hand fast in the air, I open the screen so they can see me. I still feel the gun to my head, tears are running down my face…scared, so scared… I feel a hand grab my arm, my daughter is being pulled from my arms, everythin is happening so fast now, so fast, I don't know what's going on…

Is he grabbing me back in…Did I drop my baby from my arms…?

Whats goin on, everything is moving so fast , so fast the door slams hard behind me, It's SWAT… grabbing me , came from behind my Durango, parked in the driveway, I'm screaming, fighting them off of me, I see, SWAT carrying, running with Najah in their arms…

Me- "NO MY KIDS ARE STILL IN THERE! , HE'S STILL IN THERE WITH MY KIDS , HE'S GONNA KILL MY DAUGHTER, HE BLAMES HER FOR EVERYTHING,PLEASE LET ME GO GET MY KIDS!"

I'm screaming, I'm crying, they pick me up and are carrying me down to the opposite end of me street, u can't see my house
"we're going in now m'am", they tell me.
I'm screaming, hysterical, crying...
A lot of people behind baracades, neighbors , family, news crews, police , SWAT, Everywhere.
I can't get to my family, they sit me down in front of an unfamiliar house, they hand me Najah, offer me water.
Police officers are surrounding me, I can't see anything, I'm screaming, crying.

"PLEASE LET ME GET MY KIDS, PLEASE HELLLPP ME!!!!! OH MY GOD, PLEEEEEASEE HELPPP ME!!!!
"Calm down ma'm, let us do our job" Everything is gonna be ok" WE don't want to have to remove you from the scene, please try to relax"
I'm sitting on the ground, rocking, crying, I'm itching...HI'ves I think...my feet, my neck, my face...I'm scratching, rocking, crying....
Whats takin soo long.?" Where my babies, you said they were going in, WHERE ARE MY KIDS!!OH MY GOD! PLEEEASSE HELP MEEE,GOOD GET MY KIDS!!"
Hysterical again, I am . They...didn't...go...in...
I have no idea how much time has passed.
G U N S H O T !!! LOUD OH SO LOUD.
Walkie Talkies, police voices...
SHOT FIRED! SHOTS FIRED!
I SCREAAMMM! "OHHH MYYY GODDD!
I fall hard to the ground, Bang my head, my face, my mouth.
SCREAMING, I'M SCREAMING, I'M SCREAMING!
Voices...Walkie talkie,...
"We have the girl, we have the girl!"

I look up...I'mani
They're carrying her to me shes crying, she has blood all over the front of her cloths
My Mind-"OH MY GOD, IS SHE SHOT! WHERES MY SON! WHERES MY BABY! DID HE KILL MY SON! DID HE KILL MY BABY!
They give I'mani to me.
Shes crying, shes shaking...I grab her close to me, were both crying, shaking.
I'maniI'mommyy, mommmyyy,,
Me-Wheres Akil...did he shoot Akil?, Wheres Nailah"?
"Mommmyyy, he raped me mommyy, he raped me mommyyy"
Shes crying, like I've never heard her cry before...Unexplainable sound it was.
I stop crying for some reason...I take her by her shoulders and push her in front of me to in her face to make sure I'm hearing her correctly.
"He did what!?"
I'mani- yes mommyyy, and it hurt sooo baad mommyy, it hurt sooo bad"
Crying, crying, crying
I squeeze her to me so tightly...
"Oh my god baby, I'm sooo sorry. Baby, I'm sooo sorry"
Screaming Me-"KILL HIM, YOU BETTER KILL HIM HE RAPED MY FUCKIN DAUGHTER...! YOU. SAID YOU WERE GOING IN AND HE RAPED MY BABY GIRL1"
I'mani-"he let Akil out of the bathroom after he raped me, he told Akil he was gonna kill him, he wrapped your curling iron cord around his neck. Akil asked him if he could say goodbye to his sisters first, he stopped and Akil looked at me, mouthed the word run, then out loud said
"Goodbye I'mani"

He put his attention back to Akil, he never closed the door back all the way from when he walked you out, I slipped thru the door and I ran mommy, he shot at me, when I ran out the door.

Me-"Whats the blood I'mani, did you get hit, whats the blood from"?

I'mani- "I have my period mommy, the blood is from when he was on top of me mommmmyyyy", "mommmyy, mommmyyy"

Crying, crying, crying, crying

I'm holding her close to me, crying quietly, tears rolling down my face theres no sound.

An officer approaches us, says they need to take I'mani to get checked out, my mom will go with her so I can stay on scene. They walk us over to where a van is parked, we get inside, they tell me at this point they have made phone contact and my son Akil is doing a good job, keeping them updated, and keeping. Dave some what calm.

So many peoples, so many people. I see out the window of the van, they are bringing my mom past the barricades. So she can go with I'mani. I see some of my other family members behind the barricades. My oldest son Majesty.

An officer brings my mot=m to the van, she asks if I'm ok, shes beencrying, her eyes are red and puffy, I nod my head yes, she hugs I'mani, an officer escorts I'mani and my mom to a car, and will be taken to get

Checked out. I later find out she was taken to CHILDHELP. An agency for children who have been sexually abused or molested. Since she is only 14 I'm assuming this why they took her there instead of to a regular hospital. I don't know how that all works.

An officer comes to the van, tells me they need to take my statement. They bring me over to the

other side of the street to a police RV. Theres a table inside of it. Police are inside, detectI'ves. Etc.
They sit me down at the table, gave me water, and recorded my statement.
At this point, I have no idea how much time has passed…feels like day have gone by.
They escort me out the van, and allow me to hug my oldest son. My emotions have calmed down for a while, until I embrace my son.
Majesty-"Don't cry mom, It's gonna be ok. I spoke to him on the phone. He promised hes not gonna hurt Akil, and Nailah is fine. Akil has been feeding her."
Me-"you heard what he did to I'mani right?"
Couldn't bring myself to repeat the act It'self.
Maj- "yeah, mom I know, shes gonna be ok"
An agent comes over to me and says that they have been communicating with Akil and Dave on the phne, said that Dave's emotions have been up and down all day, and has been vacilitating on if he gonna come out. The agent said that Dave has been asking to speak with me, so they made him a deal, that if they allowed me to speak with him he would come out afterwards/
I was not happy with this at all, but I wanted my kids. I'm numb, I think at this pint, I don't know what I'm feeling…
The agent wals me to a burgundy car, she hands me a notepad, written on it is what they want me to say to him. They advised me to do my best to stay calm, and to not antagonize him in anyway.
Notepad-
"Are you ok?
How are you feeling?
Do you need anything?"

No questions about my kids anywhere on the fuckin pad!
I'm angry, but I just say ok.
They give me the phone.
Me- "Dave, It's me are you ok?"
Him- "Ah, who dis?.....dis not Tasha
Me- "Dave, it is me, It's Tasha, are you ok?
I'm looking at these officers and shaking my head, they can hear the conversation, he doesn't believe It's me because I wouldn't say no shit like this to him. He know how I am when I'm upset, I was with him for 6 years.
Him- "Tash don' talk like dat, why yuh sounds so??"
Me- "Dave this is me man! This has gone on long enough . please… let the kids go and come out"
My mind- Yes, I went off script. Got me asking this muthafuckin anI'mal if hes ok, fuck him, let my kids out muthafucka,then kill yourself.!
The phone is quiet, he doesn't respond, I don't know if he still doesn't believe It's me, or what, but he says nothing
Me- "Dave?.....can I tal to Akil, is he ok hows Nailah? I need to see my son and hold my baby, she needs me. Dave, please let Akil bring Nailah out to me."
Him- "yuh know they gonna shot me down as soon as mi a come out"
His voice sounds different, not the accent, but the sound, he doesn't sound like the man I know…
Hes hoarse a little, sounds worn, maybe hes crying. I don't know. But he sounds different/
I look at the agents for some sort of a confirmation of what he believes is gonna happen if he come out.
The agent writes on the notepad, to tell him no one is going to hurt him.

I actually was already saying this too him before they wrote it, they were taking to long to give me anything.
Me-"Theyre not gonna hurt you Dave, nobody is gonna hurt you this really has gone on too long.
Him- (quietly) "ok"
The agent motions me to give her the phone I do that.
Agent- " ok Dave, we kept our promise, now you have to keep yours. Youre gonna come out now right?"
Hangs up phone.
Agent- ok, so he has agreed to come out, I guess well wait and see, hes been playing this game all day, I think hes ready though, he sounds defeated and tired."
Me- "Can I go up there with the officers?"
Agent- "yes, you can go up to the barricades and stand next to officers, don't say anything…
I stood by the barricades and waited…waited…waited
I hear shouting now…
I see Akil coming out his hands are up he has on his Elmo pajama pants, officers retrieve him and put him to the side… I don't see my baby…wheres my baby…?

"Akil! Akil!! I'm yelling his name.
They have him in custody, I hear him them say.
A SWAT team member comes over to and says that Daves is asking to talk to me again, and that they "promised" him that they would give him that opportunity. I was escorted by two SWAT team members, one on each side of me. As I'm walking towards my house, I see an ambulance. Akil and Nailah are inside being checked out by EMT's. There are several police cars parked sporadically

throughout the block in front of my house. As I get closer to my house, I start to feel sick to my stomach like I want to throw up. I'm rubbing my stomach.

They bring me to the squad, like I want t throw up. I'm rubbing my stomach.

They bring me to the squad car where Dave is inside, they advise me again not to antagonize or irritate him.

My mind- What the fuck is wrong with these people? This piece of shit just tried to kill off my whole family and raped my baby girl!! Shes never gonna be the same again!. None of us will be!

I'm standing at the squad car wit the same officers on both sides of me, standing uncomfortably close at that. Dave is looking at me through the window of he car, there is a cage on the window, I stand there and just look at him... He has tears in his eyes, mine have sensc dried up... I stand and just stare...waiting to see what this muthacucka has to say for himself.

Him- "why did you have that man in my house with my family?...that's my family." He;s snifiling and whimpering

My mind- You stupid piece of shit, are you fuckin kidding me? That's what the fuck you gotta say...! Not "I'm sorry, I don't know what I was thinking "Muthafucka I should spin in you fuckin face right now, I wanna fuckin choke you until your eyes pop out and I hear you take your last fuckin breath!!

I say nothing...

I turn to officers and ask if I can go to my kids now.

They bring me away from the car and over to the ambulance where my kids are. I clI'mb inside and hug and kiss Akil sooo tight, EMTs are taking Nailahs vitals and making sure she is ok.

Akil- "Yo this is crazy ma, I'm glad I'm out of there"

Me- "Oh my God baby, me too...You did a great job, you were so calm and brave, I'm so proud of you. You saved your sisters life"

Akil- "Where's I'mani at, I need to see my sister!

Me- Shes with grandma, they took her from the scene to be checked out, do you know what he did to her?

Akil- "yeah" he puts his head down a little. "Maj told me."

I hug him again

They hand me my baby I kiss her, and kiss her, and squeeze her tight.

They tell me that I can go in the house and get what I need for the baby as they want to take her to the hospital as a precaution.

I really don't even want to go inside the house. My family members that are still on scene stay with Nailah and Akil while I go inside the house. The street is starting to clear up from all the excessI've law enforcement. Families are allowed to go back to their homes.

I go inside my house... It's chaos inside...glass everywhere, police an investigators are inside collecting evidence. I see the gun..., I see my comforter with my little girls blood on it...pictures are being taken. I feel like I'm watching a movie, but this is really happening. I feel like I can't breather again... I grab some diapers, baby formula, water, and searching for Nailah's car seat. I go to the living room, the couches are moved around sporadically in the room...that's when I saw the top corner of my sofa was missing...a whole chick of the couch...just gone...i

then saw the bullet lodged in the front door. That's when he shot at my baby as she ran for her life...Wow!...He really shot at my baby girl...and was very close to hitting her too, looking at where the bullet lodged, she opened the door and got put in the right amount of time.
I can't believe whats happened today at all.
I grab the rest of my babies stuff... Officers told me that they would be there processing throughout the night can return tomorrow.
I ride in the ambulance to Phoenix Childrens hospital, my aunt met us there. Everyone is really quiet.
Hospital staff is polite and sympathetic. Everythng checks out well, and we drive to my sisters house. Some family are there... I'mani comes running to me and Akil, we all hug. My sister gets up and hugs me...
The TV is on and the story is all over the news. This is when I find out the whole event was 9 hours.
As everyone sat around and talked about the events of the day,... I got a cigarette from my sister, went to her backyard just sat...starin in the sky...kinda talking to God and myself...trying to understand I guess what just happened to my family.
I smiled to myself, and said "it is what is"
Went back inside, every one still talking about it, family from New York calling. I'm numb I'm over it.
I say to everyone in the room
Oh ok enough already were not gonna cry over it, were alive. That's all that matters now, lets move one.'
Everyone is looking at me crazy make me a drink...some Raspberry Vodka, get another cigarette and go back outside. I just stand there,

with my back to the door, just staring into space…at nothing in particular…..
My sister and brother in law come out…
"you ok sis?"
I don't turn around…I nod my head…
Me- "I will be .
I have never been the same again…
I don't cry, I show nothing…
My children have never been the same again…
We continue to move on with our l'ves as if nothing happened. We are close.
After all was said and done… My daughter did not want to have to testify…they offered a plea deal, which at first the muthafucka turned down…when they advised him of what he would get if we testified…he took a pleas…OF 37 YEARS. No chance for parole…just 37 years.
They tried to say he was Bipolar…after they evaluated him in the jail.
Yeah…ok…
It's over and we survived.
I play the day over and over a lot in my head, always thinking what could of happened…
Everyday is a struggle…I know have several diagnosis, and medication that I should be taking.
My children and I have been through therapy and such…
Thinks like this don't go away from therapy, or from a pill…
It is part of the skin that covers every inch of you…it breaks through to your soul…and becomes you Everyday, I struggle through the pain that I have suffered…not just from October 1, 2011… but from years of physical, sexual, and emotional abuse, brought on from the people who have claimed to love me…I am working to rebuild

myself…as I have felt broken and damaged for so long…

I can say that out of all the pain that I have suffered, good things have come from it all…the best and greatest parts of me… My 5 Beautiful children…they are the most Important, and have been my strongest supporters. I love them more than anything!

I see my therapist regularly…and continue to work through my pain in my writing.

Thank you for allowing me to share some parts of my pain, my hurts, my love, my souln…
My Life

●

I fall in love with the chaos…
The mess and the disaster inside…
Because this is what I know to be true…

●

Wake up

Wake up

Wake up

Girl what's wrong with you
You just gonna sleep through alarm clocks, Go
through stop lights, and Do not enter signs
How many lessons do you have to learn before
you wake up at the right time
And get in the right line...
The loving you and your life line
The you're beautiful, you deserve better line

Wake up

Wake up

Wake up

●

Erasing the emotions out of me

Silencing the screams
of someone please love me

Forgetting the love that never was

You're welcome to those who are walking
around with the stolen pieces of me

But, fuck you for leaving me broken.

●

Cowering to my insecurities
Enclosed like an envelope
marked return to sender
Compliments unaccepted
from anyone who may render
A kind word spoken or even written on a letter
unopened

●

People don't grow apart

People stop being honest
and stop putting in effort

People start wondering about what could happen
with someone else

●

I'm screaming, but nobody hears me
The worst pain in the world is…
Loneliness and rejection...

Love is like air….
And I cannot breathe...

I used to wanna be the rhythm you danced to...
The rhythm that moved your soul...
Now I'm realizing the record keeps skipping and
your moves are outta control...
I used to wanna be the music
that was inside your heart

Now I'm realizing that your heart is non-existent
and your soul is pretty dark...

You're fumbling over dance moves
with two left feet
Missing most steps and can't keep the beat…
I used to wanna be the rhythm you danced to...

But that rhythm you're dancing to…

Is a rhythm I just can't do.

I invited the devil into my bed over and over
And somehow expected not to get burned
I invited the devil into my heart, somehow
Expecting I wouldn't yearn...
But when I invited the devil into my soul...
A catastrophe of events took toll...
And everything that was good in me…

That devil took hold…

He broke, twisted and turned…
Then sat back and smirked
at all that he'd done...

Proud that he got, yet another one...

Snatched my heart out of my chest...

And watched mercifully as I engulfed into
flames, and inhaled the essence
of my burning flesh...

I invited the devil…

So how did I expect any less...

●

Because you feel it doesn't mean it there
I feel you touch me and you're not with me
I see your face when you're in my presence... but
you're not present
I hear you talking…
but you're not really saying anything...
I lay on your chest…you're breathing…
But your heart…is not beating...

●

You not loving me
wasn't the most painful part…

It was you not wanting me
to love you either...

●

I hate that I'm scarred…
more than most may k now…
I know I miss out on a lot of possibilities of the
things I crave and want the most…

LOVE

●

It's unfortunate and it kills me daily because I know I miss out on being loved…

I hate my scars…
I hate that I'm so badly bruised and broken that my insecurities get in the way

And I can't even recognize my worth…

●

Silenced are the screams from abuse unseen

Clenched fists that batter
a voice for help of escape

Trapped in a cage full of rage and tyranny

Covered scars, broken jaws

Isolated

Lonely

Just Kill Me Already!!!

My body shakes from his touch...

His kisses, they melt me
and I can never get enough

The soft whispers in my ear...while you're
rockin my body, is all I wanna hear

Pulling me in deeper and deeper...

My body gives in quick, when you whisper to me
"cum all over this dick"

As I try to recover...and gather my senses...

Going thru my mind is
"what an amazing lover"

This nigga right here...

Can I keep him?

●

I love you…
Will never escape my lips again
My heart can no longer sustain
Fakeness has become the norm
I'm starting to believe that LOVE
is just a word for some?
And hard to obtain
What's really real
I never thought I'd have to pretend
or hide what I feel
Settling for situations instead
of building relationships
Or even friendships have sailed away
like sinking ships
In this world full of fake shit

●

Distraction is what I have to find now
To keep myself from thinking about you
Worrying about you
Caring about you
Distraction now is what I have to find

●

Overwhelming sense of sadness...

A never ending feeling of grief

The never ending grief of myself

A hole that gets deeper and deeper

A loneliness that's constant

An emptiness that never gets filled

No one will ever understand

●

There are time when you feel lost because you
want people to agree with everything you say,
even when as your speaking you know not all of
what you are saying is agreeable…

Perception…experiences…revelation… and even
sometimes ignorance…plays a big
Part in why your journey
may be harder and longer.

●

I must learn to love myself as I am…

Do not ridicule myself due to past relationships
in my life, nor justify the wrong doings from
others as my own fault.

Do not cower to my insecurities…

Embrace the beauty who I am.

I am not perfect , but I am perfectly me.

Natasha Traceen Tolbert

Author's Notes

I'm definitely on a journey... I'm far from perfect and that's really not my goal. I strive to always be as honest with myself before anything... I fall, I make mistakes... I don't have all the answers... but I'm searching for them, and I know that I can only find those answers within myself. Am I survivor of many things...Absofuckinlutely! But even though I've survived and thrived through those things, does not take away from me being human...a woman... A vulnerable, sensitive woman at that. I am strong to a certain extent..., I get weak... I get tired... and I get lonely... and I'm searching. And on some days I search in the wrong places and I'm not ashamed of that at all. I'm hoping that more women, or just people in general, really start to be honest with themselves, and really just embrace every inch of who they are... bad or good.

We get in these dark places...and It's ok to sit in it for a little while to process... but you're supposed to stay there. If you're not ok...It's ok to say just that... if you made a bad decision... It's ok to admit that... you don't have to shout it to the world.... But there is someone that might be able to pull you out that darkness...and give you that ONE jewel that will spark something in you and understand enough to help you push through one more day. I'm on a journey with myself... and I know that my travels are long....and my walk is far from over...

I remember a time when I didn't allow people to cry around me. I mean I would literally tell them that if they were about to cry, they would have to leave or get it together. I remember as I started to heal a little, and looking at myself I realized how horrible that was to do to somebody. Who am I to stop someone's emotions.... When it hit me and I realized I have been doing it for so long...I cried.

I remember a very close friend of mine, someone I considered my family, came to my house to talk to me about something she was going through, which most people did with me..., and as she was telling me what she was dealing with, she started to cry, while she was talking, and in the middle of her telling me about this heartbreak she was currently dealing with, she literally apologized to me for crying. Holy Shit! what in the entire fuck just happened?? I couldn't believe it, and it was in that moment I knew I had a lot of work to do on myself. I told her not to apologize and that I was sorry. She laid in my lap and cried and cried and cried... She felt so much better after letting it all out. I, however felt like a piece of shit. I didn't allow the people that I claimed to care for to grieve or to feel comfortable expressing their true emotions. And here I was thinking I was a good friend... a good person... a good mother.

I didn't even allow my kids to really grieve after the hostage. In my mind, it was over, we were alive and we needed to get on with life. I had a problem with showing certain emotions for a long time, especially crying. It came from one of my relationships, where he would call me "a fuckin big baby". He would have my kids watch me while I was crying, and say "look at her, look at your mother? Aren't you guys supposed to be the babies." Mind you it was usually after he put his hands on me. It was that, and if I cried to loud

from him hitting me, he would cover my mouth so hard with his hands, or put a pillow over my face until I stopped. So I swore off crying. For me. And I honestly just couldn't handle when people cried around me. I didn't k now how to respond and it made me feel very uncomfortable. When I started to allow myself to cry again... I would do it alone only.   In the car driving home, in the shower, or just at night when everyone was asleep. I was a closet crier.
Now, I cry alone, in front of people, I don't care. And I speak on every single emotion I feel.

Hurt, embarrassed, ashamed, foolish, all of it, and I'm grateful that I have people in my life that allow me to do that. I also remember when I myself became abusive…In a relationship with someone who I used for my own selfish reasons...I thought because this guy in particular, was not the type of guy I'd usually date, he would be safe, and that he wouldn't hurt me... And I was wrong. He didn't hurt me physically, but emotionally he did. I felt like he tricked me. As he wasn't who he portrayed himself to be. And that made me angrier than I already was. I wasn't able to communicate properly, and my ego was more than bruised. I became verbally aggressive, physically aggressive, and numb to any type of loving feeling. Deep down I didn't like who I had become, and obviously had to let that relationship go before things got any worse. I made up all kinds of reasons why I felt that he deserved everything I did to him. I mean he was a liar, a manipulator, a fraud, and had me to believe he was a good man, and not like the others who had hurt me in the past. So how dare he! Right. I was so hurt inside that I wanted to share that with someone, shit, anyone. I gave zero fucks! And a part of me felt like it was my Karma, that he ended up hurting me, because I was using him. Not really in love with him, and just being with him because I thought "he was safe". It was an ugly break-up too... he talked about me to people, told them I was crazy, abusive, bipolar, and I didn't take my medicine. Funny thing was, I wasn't even mad that he did that. Initially I laughed and was like 'good, I'm glad he warned everybody who I am, so if they wanna come for me they better come ready for war, punk ass". But honestly, I couldn't be mad, because what he was saying was true. I behaved like that towards him, no matter how I try to justify why I did it, the bottom line was I did it, and it was wrong. My kids watched me throw things at this man, physically attack him, spit at him, call him all types of names... I literally became the same person that I moved a thousand mile to get away from. A disgusting, horrible, angry, mean and ugly person.

Domestic violence is a very serious subject and hard to talk about at times... especially when you get that million-dollar question.... "why didn't you leave?" Anybody who has experienced domestic violence or any situation of abuse will have an answer that nobody will understand unless they've experienced it.

My thing initially, yes, "I love him", then the next thing was, I wanted a whole family. I didn't grow up with my dad and never really got to know him before he passed away. I didn't want that for my children. However, he wasn't even a good father. Another thing for me was I had 3 children at that time,and my oldest son had a different father, so in my mind, I also didn't want to be "that girl" with a bunch of different baby daddies, or no real father figure , or a "whole family". Which ultI'mately ended up being the exact case. I've raised my 5 children alone... and I have 3 baby daddies... 2 which hurt me in the most unI'maginable ways... I hold guilt inside because of what my children endured, as well as emotional instability, insecurities, emptiness, and this unexplainable gut wrenching hurt inside of myself. These things hinder me greatly. I find myself still at 42 years old struggling with insecurities and trying to understand, first of all why these things happened. And because these feelings are still there at times, I find myself in these 'relationships" or "situationships" that are very unhealthy for me. Not necessarily on a physical abusive level, but on a very deep emotional level. Even when I recognize it, something in me still has a hard time letting it go and moving forward. Which is insane. I go through these phases of growth, then those insecurities creep up on me and I get stuck there. And I get a lot of intrusive, self-loathing thoughts about myself and beat myself up probably more than any man has ever done. Even as I know what I'm doing to myself, something in me can't stop it. I sit in that phase for a while, never really knowing when I'm gonna snap out of it and get my life together. Then whenever that phase is finally over... I go through another growth spurt of self-love and acknowledgement for myself and how far I've come from those situations. I'm also able to recognize the part I played in those situations, by expecting people to be something that they are not, or incapable of at that moment.

Some people have not grown to their own full potential.

I realize that just because you have a connection with someone does not mean you're fully compatible. Emotional and spiritual compatibility is also very Important.

Thank you for reading my journey through poetry and prose and thank you for allowing me to share my scars... beautiful scars.

●

Made in the USA
Middletown, DE
06 July 2019